First Facts

American Symbols

The Liberty Bell

by Debbie L. Yanuck

Consultant:
Melodie Andrews, Ph.D.
Associate Professor of Early American History
Minnesota State University, Mankato

Capstone

Capstone Press
151 Good Counsel Drive, P.O. Box 669, Mankato, Minnesota 56002
http://www.capstone-press.com

Library of Congress Cataloging-in-Publication Data
Yanuck, Debbie L.
    The Liberty Bell / by Debbie L. Yanuck.
        v. cm.—(American symbols)
    Includes bibliographical references and index.
    Contents: Liberty Bell fast facts—American symbol of freedom—A new bell—The bell
cracks—Fixing the bell—The bell cracks again—The Libery Bell tours America—The
Liberty Bell today—Timeline—Hands On: The Liberty Bell Game.
    ISBN 0-7368-1630-5 (hardcover)
    1. Liberty Bell—Juvenile literature. 2. Philadelphia (Pa.)—Buildings, structures, etc.—
Juvenile literature. [1. Liberty Bell. 2. Philadelphia (Pa.)—Buildings, structures, etc.] I. Title.
II. American symbols (Mankato, Minn.)
F158.8.I3 .Y36 2003
974.8'11—dc21   2002010707

Summary: Discusses the history of the Liberty Bell, its construction, its reconstruction, its
    location, and its importance as a symbol of the United States.

Editorial Credits
Chris Harbo and Roberta Schmidt, editors; Eric Kudalis, product planning editor;
    Linda Clavel, cover and interior designer; Alta Schaffer, photo researcher

Photo Credits
Corbis/Bob Krist, 19
Independence National Historic Park, 5, 13, 17, 21
Photo Network/Henryk T. Kaiser, cover; Jeff Greenberg, 11
Photri-Microstock, 8
Stock Montage, Inc., 7, 20
Visuals Unlimited/John D. Cunningham, 15

1 2 3 4 5 6 08 07 06 05 04 03

Table of Contents

Liberty Bell Fast Facts. 4

American Symbol of Freedom 6

A New Bell. 8

The Bell Cracks 10

Fixing the Bell 12

The Bell Cracks Again. 14

The Liberty Bell Tours the United States. 16

The Liberty Bell Today 18

Timeline 20

Hands On: The Liberty Bell Game. 22

Words to Know 23

Read More 24

Internet Sites 24

Index. 24

Liberty Bell Fast Facts

- The Liberty Bell was ordered from England in 1751.

- In 1753, the Liberty Bell cracked the first time it was rung.

- John Pass and John Stow fixed the Liberty Bell twice in 1753.

- The Liberty Bell rang at the reading of the Declaration of Independence in 1776.

- In 1839, the Liberty Bell got its name from a booklet against slavery. This booklet used a drawing of the bell as a symbol of freedom.

- The Liberty Bell traveled around the United States between 1885 and 1915.

5

American Symbol of Freedom

The Liberty Bell is a symbol of freedom. On July 8, 1776, it rang in Philadelphia, Pennsylvania. People gathered to hear the Declaration of Independence read aloud for the first time. People rang the Liberty Bell to announce America's independence from Great Britain.

Declaration of Independence

a paper that said the 13 American colonies were free from British rule

In the 1700s, bells announced meetings and warned people of danger. In 1751, the State House in Philadelphia needed a new bell.

Location of the Liberty Bell

Nobody in America made bells. A large copper bell was ordered from England. It weighed 2,080 pounds (943 kilograms).

The Bell Cracks

In September 1752, the Liberty Bell arrived in America by ship. In March 1753, the bell was hung on a stand in front of the State House. People wanted to hear the bell ring. They pulled the clapper. The Liberty Bell rang once and cracked.

clapper
the swinging piece of metal inside a bell that makes it ring

Fixing the Bell

John Pass and John Stow were hired to fix the bell. They melted the bell down. They reshaped the bell in a mold. The new bell made a dull sound. Pass and Stow melted the bell down again. In June 1753, they hung the finished bell in the State House tower.

mold
a container used to shape something

… OF LEV. XXV. V X. PROCLAIM L…
…E IN PHILADᴬ. BY ORDER OF…

PASS AND STOW
PHILADᴬ
MDCCLIII

The Bell Cracks Again

The Liberty Bell rang for many important events. Then in 1835, the bell cracked again. In 1846, workers fixed the crack. That year, the bell rang to celebrate George Washington's birthday. It cracked worse than before. The Liberty Bell never rang again.

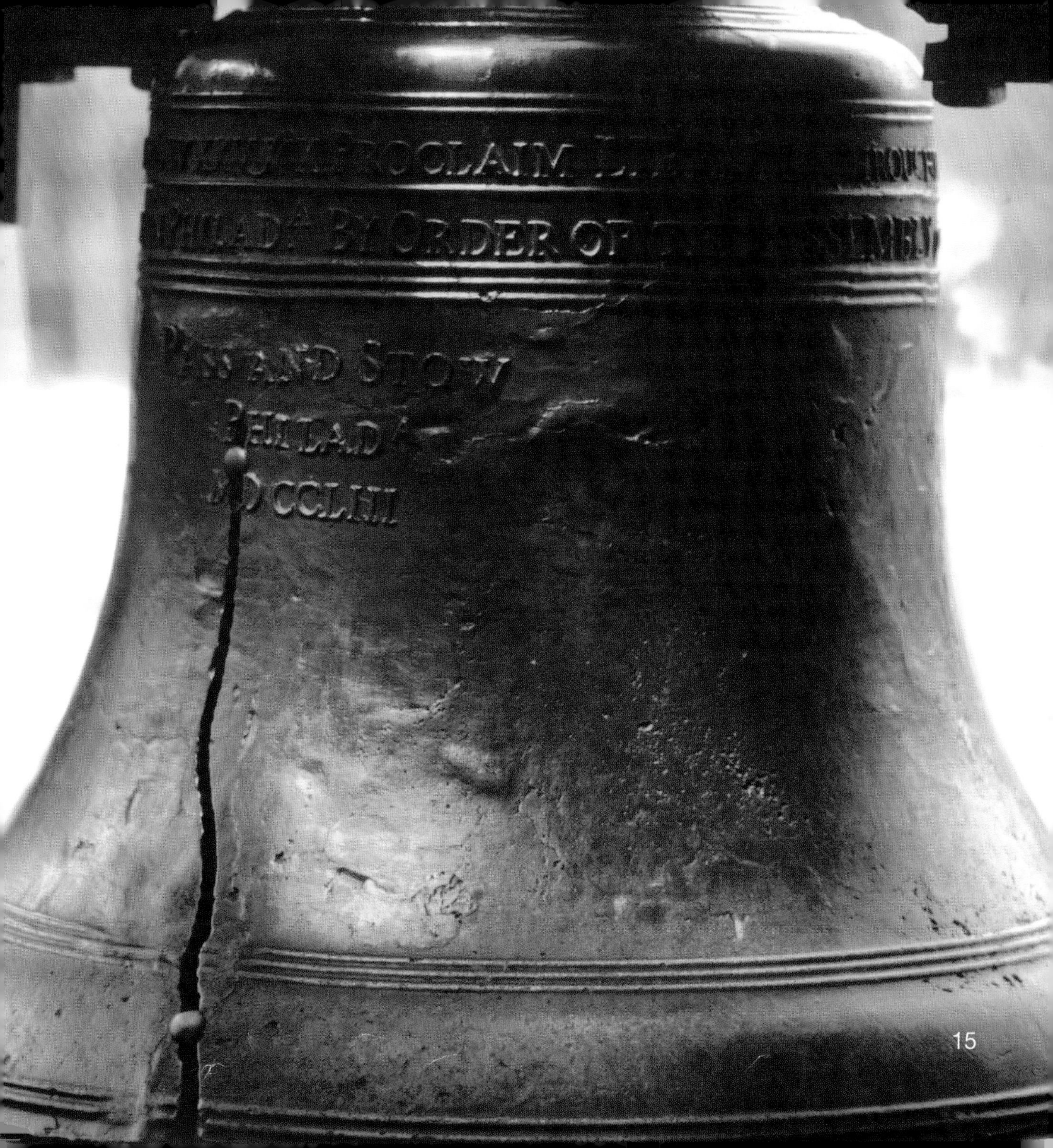
PROCLAIM
BY ORDER OF
PASS AND STOW

The Liberty Bell Tours the United States

In 1885, the Liberty Bell began to tour
the United States. It traveled by railroad
to fairs across the country. The bell
made seven trips across the United
States. It stopped in nearly 400 cities.
At each stop, many people came to see
the Liberty Bell.

The Liberty Bell Today

Today, the Liberty Bell is on display near Independence Hall. Independence Hall is now the name for the State House. Each Fourth of July, the Liberty Bell is gently tapped with a rubber hammer. The bell is struck to honor America's freedom.

Timeline

1753—The Liberty Bell cracks the first time it rings.

1776—The Liberty Bell rings at the first public reading of the Declaration of Independence on July 8.

1751—The Liberty Bell is ordered from England.

1753—Pass and Stow fix the bell twice.

1846—Workers fix the Liberty Bell for George Washington's birthday. The bell cracks again.

1976—The Liberty Bell moves to a building across the street from Independence Hall.

1835—The Liberty Bell cracks again.

1885—The Liberty Bell begins to travel around the United States.

Hands On: The Liberty Bell Game

In 1751, the Liberty Bell was ordered from England. The bell traveled across the Atlantic Ocean by ship. Play a game to get the Liberty Bell from the ship to Independence Hall.

What You Need

White sheet of paper   Penny
Colored pencils   Chocolate kisses candy

What You Do

1. Draw a small square in the top right-hand corner of the paper. Write "Independence Hall" underneath the square.
2. Draw a small triangle in the bottom left-hand corner of the paper. Write "ship" underneath the triangle.
3. Use the penny to trace 15 circles from the triangle to the square. Write the word "cracked" in three circles along the path.
4. Each player takes one chocolate kiss candy. This is your bell. Put the bells on the boat.
5. Decide who will go first. The player to go first spins the penny. If the penny lands face up, the player moves his or her bell forward two circles. If the penny lands face down, the player moves back one circle. If the bell lands on a circle with the word "cracked," that player moves back three circles.
6. Take turns spinning the penny. The first person to reach Independence Hall wins the game.

Words to Know

announce (uh-NOUNSS)—to tell people something in public

clapper (KLAP-ur)—a swinging piece of metal that makes a bell ring

colony (KOL-uh-nee)—an area that has been settled by people from another country; a colony is ruled by another country.

copper (KOP-ur)—a reddish brown metal

freedom (FREE-duhm)—the right to live the way you want

independence (in-di-PEN-duhnss)—freedom from the control of other people or things

liberty (LIB-ur-tee)—freedom

symbol (SIM-buhl)—an object that stands for something else

tour (TOOR)—to take a trip to different places

Read More

Binns, Tristan Boyer. *The Liberty Bell.* Symbols of Freedom. Chicago: Heinemann, 2001.

Wilson, Jon. *The Liberty Bell: The Sounds of Freedom.* Chanhassen, Minn.: Child's World, 1999.

Internet Sites

Track down many sites about the Liberty Bell.

Visit the FACT HOUND at
http://www.facthound.com

IT IS EASY! IT IS FUN!

1) Go to *http://www.facthound.com*
2) Type in: 0736816305
3) Click on "FETCH IT" and FACT HOUND will find several links hand-picked by our editors.

Relax and let our pal FACT HOUND do the research for you!

Index

clapper, 10
colonies, 6
Declaration of Independence, 6
England, 9
freedom, 6, 18
Independence Hall, 18

Pass, John, 12
Philadelphia, Pennsylvania, 6, 8
State House, 8, 10, 12
Stow, John, 12
tour, 16
Washington, George, 14